EASA Private Pilot Licence
Aeroplane & Helicopter
Meteorology Revision Guide

ISBN 9781906 559397

Airplan Flight Equipment

This book is intended to be a study aid to the Meteorology Theoretical Knowledge element of the EASA PPL (A & H) course. It does not in any way replace or overrule the instruction you will receive from a flight instructor at an approved or registered training organisation.

Nothing in this publication overrules or supersedes EASA regulations or EU rules and other documents published by a competent authority; the flight manual/pilot's operating handbook for the aircraft being flown; the pilot order book or operations manual; training syllabus; or the general provisions of good airmanship and safe flying practice.

First Edition 2013

©Copyright 2013 AFE Ltd.

EASA Private Pilot Licence
Aeroplane & Helicopter
Meteorology Revision Guide

ISBN 9781906 559397

Airplan Flight Equipment
1a Ringway Trading Estate
Shadowmoss Road
Manchester M22 5LH
Tel: 0161 499 0023
Fax: 0161 499 0298
www.afeonline.com

CONTENTS

EASA PPL Meteorology Essential Revision   5

Meteorology Practice Paper One   14

Meteorology Practice Paper Two   20

Meteorology Practice Paper Three   26

Meteorology Paper One Answers   32

Meteorology Paper Two Answers   38

Meteorology Paper Three Answers   44

Intentionally Left Blank

The Atmosphere

Most 'weather' occurs in the **troposphere**, the layer of the atmosphere in contact with the earth.

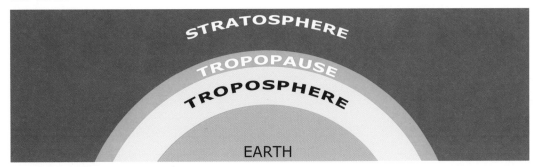

Air Temperature

The rate at which air temperature decreases with increasing altitude is called the temperature '**lapse rate**'. The temperature lapse rate in the International Standard Atmosphere is 2°C per 1000ft

Atmospheric Pressure

Atmospheric pressure decreases with increasing altitude. Atmospheric pressure is measured in aviation using the hectopascal (hPA), one hectopascal is taken as being equivalent to 30ft of altitude.

Air Density

Air density is inversely proportional to air temperature – that is, as air temperature increases, air density decreases. Air density is proportional to air pressure, as air pressure increases, air density increases.

The International Standard Atmosphere (ISA)

Surface Temperature	+15°C.
Pressure	1013·25hPa.
Temperature Lapse Rate	1·98°C/1000ft.

Altimetry

Altitude	QNH is set on the altimeter sub-scale, altitude above mean sea level is indicated.
Height	QFE is set on the altimeter sub-scale, height above a set datum is indicated.
Flight Level	1013hPa is set on the altimeter sub-scale, Flight Level above this pressure level is indicated.

If an aircraft flies from high-pressure to low-pressure without updating the altimeter setting, the altimeter will over-read (indicating that the aircraft is higher than it actually is): "**high to low, down you go**".

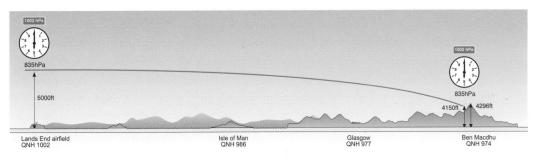

If an aircraft flies in air which is colder than ISA temperature, the altimeter will over-read, it is indicating that the aircraft is higher than its true altitude. If an aircraft flies in air which is warmer than ISA temperature, the altimeter will under-read, it is indicating that the aircraft is lower than its true altitude.

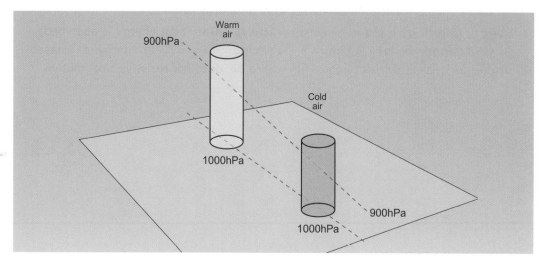

Wind

Air flows from high pressure to low pressure as a consequence of **pressure gradient force**. Moving air is deflected to the right (in the northern hemisphere) by **Coriolis Force**.

If the pressure gradient and Coriolis forces balance, the resulting air flow tends to be parallel to isobars.

Buys Ballot's Law states that in the northern hemisphere, if you stand with your back to the wind, the low-pressure area is on your left.

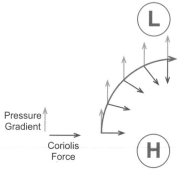

Mountain Waves

Strong airflow across a mountain range can create **mountain waves**. Where the waves turn down on the downwind or 'lee' side of the mountains the mass of descending air can force aircraft to descend, even at full power and best climb airspeed. Saucer-shaped **lenticular** clouds can form at the crests of the mountain waves.

The dangerous phenomena of 'rotor' (an area of extreme turbulence) can occur just downwind of the crest of a mountain or ridge.

Thermodynamics

Warm air can hold more water vapour than cold air. As air temperature decreases, relative humidity increases.

When water changes state, an exchange of heat energy takes place:

Solid – (*Melting*) – Liquid – (*Evaporation*) – Gas (heat energy is absorbed)

Gas – (*Condensation*) – Liquid – (*Freezing*) – Solid (heat energy is released)

Stable air resists vertical motion, **unstable air** does not resist vertical motion.

Clouds and Fog

When the air reaches its dewpoint temperature, the air is saturated, any further reduction in temperature causes the water vapour to condense into water droplets – cloud. Cloud forming on the surface is fog. Unstable air encourages vertical clouds to develop, which may give short-lived, intense precipitation. Stable air tends to contain layered clouds, which may give long-lasting but less intense precipitation.

Fog, Mist, Haze and Precipitation

Radiation fog forms only over land and is caused by surface cooling at night. The three principal factors for the formation of radiation fog are:

- Little or no cloud at night and cooling by radiation.

- High relative humidity.

- Light winds, ideally 2-8 knots.

Frontal fog can form in the prolonged precipitation ahead of a slow-moving warm or occluded front.

Air Masses and Fronts

A front is the boundary between two air masses.

A **warm front** brings warm air to replace cold air. A **cold front** brings cold air to replace warmer air.

A warm front has a frontal slope of around 1:150, cloud is layer type and precipitation tends to reach the ground 100-200nm ahead of the surface front.

A cold front has a frontal slope of around 1:50, cloud is vertical type and heavy precipitation is common.

Pressure Systems

In a low pressure system (or **depression**) air circulates anti-clockwise in the Northern Hemisphere. Low pressure systems, often contain areas of extensive cloud and precipitation. The lower the pressure at the centre of the depression, the more likely it is to contain bad weather including active fronts and strong winds.

In a high pressure system (or **anticyclone**) the air circulates clockwise in the Northern Hemisphere. An anticyclone generally features light winds and little cloud. A summer anticyclone in Europe often brings 'heatwave' weather. In spring and autumn, the slack winds and clear skies within an anticyclone can encourage the formation of radiation fog. In winter a persistent anticyclone can develop widespread low cloud and poor visibility – 'anticyclonic gloom'.

Climatology

In the summer, the predominate feature of the European climate is areas of high pressure spreading in from the mid-Atlantic ocean bringing settled weather with light winds and little precipitation.

In the winter, westerly winds tend to bring areas of low pressure from the North Atlantic, bringing extensive cloud, precipitation and at times strong winds.

The Western Europe climate is most often dominated by weather arriving from the Atlantic Ocean, the closer to the western coast, the milder the climate. In Eastern Europe, away from the influence of the Atlantic, a more continental climate prevails, with hotter summers and colder winters.

Flight Hazards

The classic environment for **rain ice** is the area just ahead of a warm front in winter.

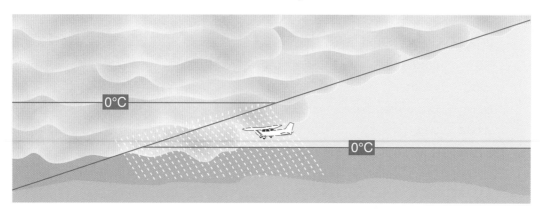

The dominant factor in **carburettor icing** is the moisture content of the air: the more humid the air, the higher the risk of carburettor icing. Carburettor icing is a particular danger at low power settings. **Hoar frost** can occur on the ground or if an aircraft descends from above the freezing level into warmer air. **Rime ice** and **clear ice** generally only occur if an aircraft is flown in cloud above the freezing level.

The three stages of a **thunderstorm's** life cycle are:

- The cumulus stage, a period of rapid vertical growth, leading to 'towering cumulus'.

- The mature stage is marked by precipitation beginning to fall from the cloud. This is the most active phase of the storm

- The dissipating stage when the top of the cloud spreads out in the characteristic anvil shape.

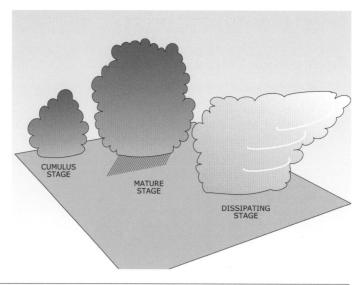

Metrological Information

A **TAF** is a fixed-period forecast of expected weather for a specific airfield. A **METAR** is an actual observation of the weather at an airfield. **VOLMET** is a recorded broadcast giving the METARs for around ten airfields in an area.

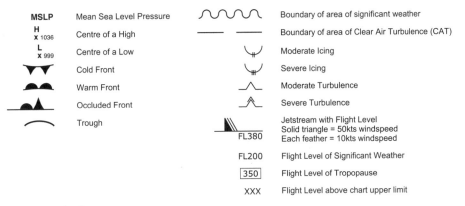

MET Symbols:

CAT	Clear Air Turbulence
CB	Cumulonimbus cloud
EMBD	Embedded in other cloud
FRQ	Frequent (hardly or not at all separated)
ISOL	Isolated
OCNL	Occasional (well separated)
WDPR	Widespread

Common weather abbreviations:

DZ drizzle	FG fog	FZ freezing
RA rain	HZ haze	SH shower
SN snow	BR mist	TS thunderstorm
GS small hail/snow pellets		
GR hail		

Prefixes:

- (eg –DZ) indicates slight precipitation.

  No prefix indicates moderate precipitation (eg RA)

+ (eg +RA) indicates heavy precipitation

Standard abbreviations for cloud type will be used:

Altocumulus	AC
Altostratus	AS
Cirrocumulus	CC
Cirrostratus	CS
Cirrus	CI
Cumulonimbus	CB
Cumulus	CU
Nimbostratus	NS
Stratocumulus	SC
Stratus	ST

METAR & TAF Codes:

METAR	Aviation Routine Weather Report
TAF	Terminal Aerodrome Forecast
AUTO	Automated METAR

SURFACE WIND

00000	Wind Calm
G	Wind Gust
KT	Knots
V	Variation in wind direction
VRB	Variable Wind Direction

VISIBILITY

9999	Visibility 10km or more
0000	Visibility less than 50m
R	RVR
N	North
NE	North East
E	East
SE	South East
S	South
SW	South West
W	West
NW	North West

WEATHER
Description:

BC	Patches
BL	Blowing
DR	Drifting
FZ	Freezing
MI	Shallow
SH	Shower(s)
TS	Thunderstorm
VCTS	Thunderstorm in the vicinity

Precipitation:

DZ	Drizzle
GR	Hail
GS	Small Hail
IC	Ice Crystals (diamond dust)
PL	Ice Pellets
RA	Rain
SG	Snow Grains
SN	Snow
UP	Unidentified Precipitation
-	Light
+	Heavy

Visibility Factor:

BR	Mist
DU	Dust
FG	Fog
FU	Smoke
HZ	Haze
PRFG	Partial Fog (fog banks)
SA	Sand
VA	Volcanic Ash

Other:

DS	Dust Storm
FC	Funnel Cloud(s) – tornado or water-spout
NSW	No Significant Weather
PO	Dust Devils
SQ	Squall(s)
SS	Sandstorm
VC	in the Vicinity

CLOUD

BKN	Broken (5-7 oktas)
FEW	Few (1-2 oktas)
OVC	Overcast (8 oktas)
SCT	Scattered (3-4 oktas)
CB	Cumulonimbus
TCU	Towering Cumulus
NCD	No Cloud Detected
NSC	No Significant Cloud
SKC	Sky Clear
VV	Sky obscured
VV///	Sky obscured, vertical visibility cannot be assessed.
CAVOK	Ceiling And Visibility OK (i) Visibility: 10km or more. (ii) Cloud: no cloud below 5000ft or below highest Minimum Sector Altitude, whichever is greater, and no CB at any height. (iii) No significant weather phenomena at, or in the vicinity of, the aerodrome.

AIR TEMPERATURE/DEW POINT

M	Minus

PRESSURE

Q	QNH

SUPPLEMENTARY INFORMATION

/////	information not available
BECMG	Becoming
NOSIG	No Significant changes forecast
PROB 30	30% Probability
PROB 40	40% Probability
RE	Recent weather
TEMPO	Temporary
TREND	Trend indicator
WS	Windshear

Intentionally Left Blank

EASA Private Pilot Licence
Aeroplane & Helicopter
Meteorology

Time allowed: 60 minutes

No. of questions: 20

Total Marks: 100

Instructions:

The paper consists of 20 multiple choice questions, each carries 5 marks. The pass mark is 75% (ie 15 questions or more must be answered correctly). Marks are not deducted for incorrect answers.

Be sure to carefully read each question and ensure that you understand it before considering the answer choices. Only one of the answers is complete and correct; the others are either incomplete, incorrect or based on a misconception.

You should indicate the correct answer by placing a cross in the appropriate box of the answer sheet. If you decide to change an answer, you should erase the original choice and put a cross in the box representing your new selection.

Each question has an average answer time of 3 minutes. No credit is given for unanswered questions

Meteorology Practice Paper ONE

1. If a strong wind is blowing across a mountain ridge, where is the strongest turbulence in 'rotor' conditions most likely to be found?

   (a) Approximately 10,000ft directly above the ridge

   (b) Upwind of the ridge

   (c) On the valley floor

   (d) Downwind of the ridge

2. A parcel of air has a relative humidity of 85%. If this parcel of air is cooled, the relative humidity can be expected to:

   (a) decrease

   (b) increase

   (c) move further away from saturation

   (d) remain unchanged

3. If the wind at 2000ft altitude is 240/35, the most likely surface wind at an inland airfield is:

   (a) 270/20

   (b) 250/40

   (c) 220/40

   (d) 220/20

4. Lenticular clouds (that is, clouds of the Lenticularus species) are most likely to form:

   (a) In a layer of fog over the sea

   (b) In calm conditiond

   (c) In orographic uplift or mountain waves

   (d) Over lakes and open water on a calm winter night

5. In western Europe, an aircraft is flying directly towards the centre of a depression at an altitude of 5000ft. If no other factors apply, which of the following statements is most likely to be correct:

   (a) The aircraft will experience drift to the right (starboard)

   (b) The aircraft will experience drift to the left (port)

   (c) The aircraft will experience a direct tailwind without drift

   (d) The aircraft will experience a direct headwind without drift

6. The ISA temperature at an altitude of 7,000ft is:

   (a) +1°C

   (b) +15°C

   (c) +4.5°C

   (d) -6°C

7. If there is no cloud cover and no change of air mass, the surface temperature is likely to be coldest at what time of day?

   (a) Midnight

   (b) 3am

   (c) Just before sunrise

   (d) Just after sunrise (dawn)

8. The great majority of 'weather' is found in the lowest level of the atmosphere, which is known as:

   (a)   The ozonesphere

   (b)   The tropopause

   (c)   The troposphere

   (d)   The stratosphere

9. Flight close to or within a thunderstorm should be avoided at all times. Nevertheless, within a cumulonimbus cloud the most severe airframe icing be expected to occur:

   (a)   Where the temperature range is between 0°C and −30°C

   (b)   Only above 10,000ft

   (c)   At the base of the cloud

   (d)   Only below 10,000ft

10. Within a depression two air masses meet so that a warm front is formed. In relation to a 'typical' warm front:

    (a)   Warm air will be replaced by cold air, the frontal slope will be around 1:150

    (b)   Cold air will be replaced by warm air, the frontal slope will be around 1:150

    (c)   Warm air will be replaced by cold air, the frontal slope will be around 1:50

    (d)   Cold air will be replaced by warm air, the frontal slope will be around 1:50

11. You are flying in rain ahead of a warm front in winter. The outside air temperature is −2°C. Which of the following meteorological phenomena is most likely to affect the aircraft?

    (a)   Tornadoes

    (b)   Hail

    (c)   Rain ice

    (d)   Radiation fog

12. An unstable air mass is forced to rise over a mountain range, which of the following is most likely?

    (a)   Extensive stratus cloud

    (b)   Radiation Fog

    (c)   Scattered cirrus cloud

    (d)   Cumuloform cloud

13. The cloud sequence that could be expected during the passage of a 'typical' warm front would be:

    (a)   CI, AS, CB, CU

    (b)   AS, NS, CI, CS, CB,

    (c)   CI, CS, AS, NS, ST

    (d)   CB, AS

14. In the UK, an unstable air mass bringing extensive convective cloud, heavy showers and possibly thunderstorms is most likely to be a:

    (a)   Polar Maritime air mass

    (b)   Polar Continental air mass

    (c)   Tropical Continental air mass

    (d)   Tropical Maritime air mass

Turn to the METFORM 214 at appendix A

15. Which of the following most closely represents the forecast wind velocity [i] and temperature [ii] at 2000ft at position 50N 00E/W?

	[i]	[ii]
(a)	280/15	+11°C
(b)	270/18	+13°C
(c)	260/20	+14°C
(d)	270/20	+11°C

Turn to the METFORM 215 at appendix B to answer the following questions:

16. The freezing level (where 0°C occurs) over the south coast of England is:

    (a)   8000ft amsl

    (b)   800ft amsl

    (c)   800ft agl

    (d)   5000ft amsl

17. In Area A within the section 'SURFACE VIS AND WX' what does the following text mean: "ISOL 4000M +SHRA/+TSGR MON N 56N":

    (a)   Occasional areas of 40.00mm precipitation, heavy showers of rain or thunderstorms with hail, over mountains north of latitude 56°N

    (b)   Isolated areas of 4000m visibility, additionally showers of rain or heavy thunderstorms above FL56 over mountains

    (c)   Isolated areas of 4000m visibility in heavy showers of rain or heavy thunderstorms with hail, above or covering mountains north of latitude 56°N in Area A

    (d)   Isolated areas may experience 40.00mm of precipitation in heavy showers of rain or thunderstorms with hail over mountains anywhere north of latitude 56N

18. What is the feature identified as [i] in the lower third of the forecast chart:

    (a)   A warm front moving south east at less than 5 knots

    (b)   A cold front moving south east at less than 5 knots

    (c)   A cold front moving north east at 5-10 knots

    (d)   A cold occlusion moving east at less than 10 knots

19. In Area A 'CLOUD' section, what does the following mean:

    "BKN CB 008 XXX ∪ ∧ "

    (a)   Broken (5-7 oktas) Cumulonimbus cloud, base 800ft above ground level, upper limit unknown, moderate icing, moderate turbulence

    (b)   Broken (5-7 oktas) Cumulus cloud, base 8000ft above ground level, upper limit unknown, moderate icing, moderate turbulence

    (c)   Broken (5-7 oktas) Cumulonimbus cloud, base 800ft above mean sea level, extending to above chart upper limit, severe icing, severe turbulence

    (d)   Broken (5-7 oktas) Cumulonimbus cloud, base 800ft above mean ground level, extending to information missing, severe icing, severe turbulence

20. Disregard airspace along the stated route for the purposes of answering this question.

A flight is planned from Coventry (A) to Newcastle (B) with alternate Durham Tees Valley (C), routing outside controlled airspace where possible and avoiding high ground.

The aircraft cannot fly in known icing conditions.

The pilot holds a PPL without instrument qualification, so the flight must be conducted under VFR.

The minimum en-route altitude will be 1000ft agl, VMC minima require that the aircraft remains clear of cloud, in sight of the surface and in a minimum flight visibility of 5km.

The estimated time of departure is 1400Z, the time en-route is two hours.

The METAR for the departure airfield 'A' at 1350Z is:

27016KT 9999 SCT020 15/8 Q1001

The TAF for the destination airfield 'B' is:

0312/0412 29015KT 9999 BKN022 TEMPO0312/0412 9000 SHRA BKN012

Considering this information, and METFORM 215 (appendix B), choose the most reasonable course of action:

(a) Cancel the flight, the forecasts indicate that the weather will be below limits with en-route visibility down to 800m in fog and cloud base down to 200ft.

(b) Delay the departure by two hours. Although the departure conditions are suitable, the destination aerodrome forecast indicates that conditions will get better after 1600, although before that the cloud base will be down to 220ft.

(c) The conditions at the departure airfield and en-route forecast are generally suitable, although there may be occasional showers en-route. The destination airfield forecast indicates that showers may occur starting at around the ETA, proceed with caution.

(d) The departure conditions indicate scattered cloud down to 200ft. Delay the departure until this cloud has cleared. Conditions at the destination are also forecast to improve after 1600 so delaying departure will allow arrival into better conditions.

Appendix A: UK Low-Level Spot Wind Chart (Form 214)

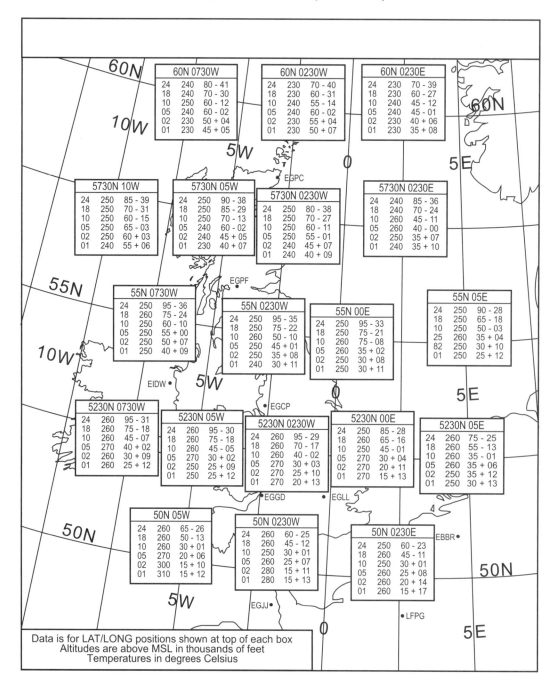

60N 0730W

24	240	80 - 41
18	240	70 - 30
10	250	60 - 12
05	240	60 - 02
02	230	50 + 04
01	230	45 + 05

60N 0230W

24	230	70 - 40
18	230	60 - 31
10	240	55 - 14
05	240	60 - 02
02	230	55 + 04
01	230	50 + 07

60N 0230E

24	230	70 - 39
18	230	60 - 27
10	240	45 - 12
05	240	45 - 01
02	230	40 + 06
01	230	35 + 08

5730N 10W

24	250	85 - 39
18	250	70 - 31
10	250	60 - 15
05	250	65 - 03
02	250	60 + 03
01	240	55 + 06

5730N 05W

24	250	90 - 38
18	250	85 - 29
10	250	70 - 13
05	240	60 - 02
02	240	45 + 05
01	230	40 + 07

5730N 0230W

24	250	80 - 38
18	250	70 - 27
10	250	60 - 11
05	250	55 - 01
02	240	45 + 07
01	240	40 + 09

5730N 0230E

24	240	85 - 36
18	240	70 - 24
10	260	45 - 11
05	260	40 - 00
02	250	35 + 07
01	240	35 + 10

55N 0730W

24	250	95 - 36
18	260	75 - 24
10	250	60 - 10
05	250	55 + 00
02	250	50 + 07
01	250	40 + 09

55N 0230W

24	250	95 - 35
18	250	75 - 22
10	260	50 - 10
05	250	45 + 01
02	250	35 + 08
01	240	30 + 11

55N 00E

24	250	95 - 33
18	250	75 - 21
10	260	75 - 08
05	250	35 + 02
02	250	30 + 08
01	250	30 + 11

55N 05E

24	250	90 - 28
18	250	65 - 18
10	250	50 - 03
25	260	35 + 04
82	250	30 + 10
01	250	25 + 12

5230N 0730W

24	260	95 - 31
18	260	75 - 18
10	260	45 - 07
05	270	40 + 02
02	260	30 + 09
01	260	25 + 12

5230N 05W

24	260	95 - 30
18	260	75 - 18
10	260	45 - 05
05	270	30 + 02
02	250	25 + 09
01	250	25 + 12

5230N 0230W

24	260	95 - 29
18	260	70 - 17
10	260	40 - 02
05	270	30 + 03
02	270	25 + 10
01	270	20 + 13

5230N 00E

24	250	85 - 28
18	260	65 - 16
10	260	45 - 01
05	270	30 + 04
02	270	20 + 11
01	270	15 + 13

5230N 05E

24	260	75 - 25
18	260	55 - 13
10	260	35 - 01
05	260	35 + 06
02	250	35 + 12
01	250	30 + 13

50N 05W

24	260	65 - 26
18	260	50 - 13
10	260	30 + 01
05	270	20 + 06
02	300	15 + 10
01	310	15 + 12

50N 0230W

24	260	60 - 25
18	260	45 - 12
10	250	30 + 01
05	260	25 + 07
02	280	15 + 11
01	280	15 + 13

50N 0230E

24	250	60 - 23
18	260	45 - 11
10	250	30 + 01
05	260	25 + 08
02	260	20 + 14
01	260	15 + 17

Data is for LAT/LONG positions shown at top of each box
Altitudes are above MSL in thousands of feet
Temperatures in degrees Celsius

Appendix B: UK Forecast Weather (Form 215)

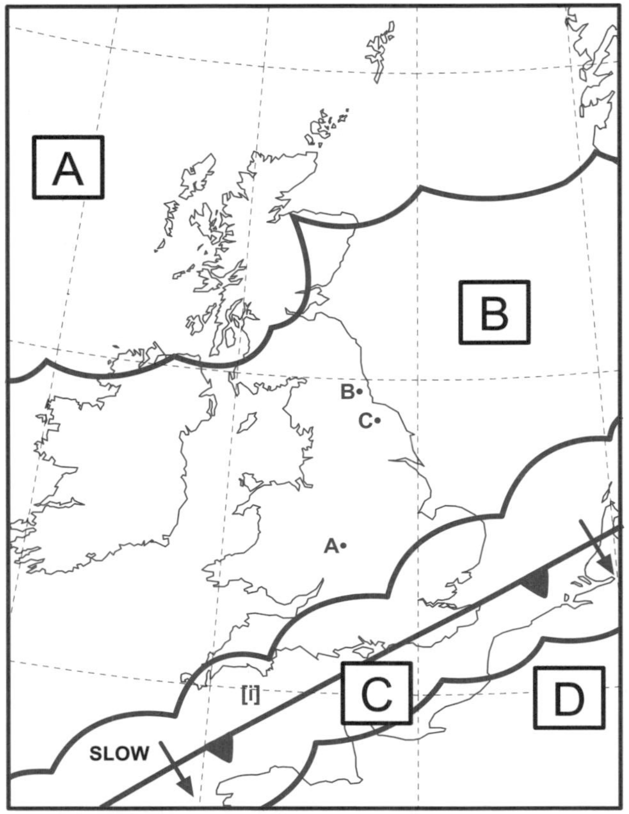

Forecast Weather

Valid 030800 to 031700 Z

Fronts/zones valid at 1200 Z

AREA	SURFACE VIS AND WX	CLOUD	0 C
A	30KM NIL FRQ 8KM SHRA ISOL 4000M +SHRA/ +TSGR MON N 56N	BKN CU SC 020 - 080 BKN CU 012 – XXX ⅂⅂ BKN CB 008 - XXX ⅂⅂	040
B	30KM NIL OCNL 10KM RA SH	SCT/BKN CU 025-060 BKN ST SC 015 – 100	050 - 080
C	10KM NIL/RA OCNL 3500M RA/DZ OCNL 800M FG/DZ	BKN ST 012-015 OVC NS 006-100 SCT/BKN SC 002 – 050	080
D	20KM NIL/RA	NIL/FEW SC 035-060	100

Outlook Until:

Similar

All heights in 100's of feet above mean sea level
XXX means above chart upper limit
Cloud amount (Oktas)   MOD / SEV ICE   Speed of movement in KT
FEW : 1-2 SCT: 3-4   MOD / SEV TURB   Temperatures in DEG C
BKN: 5-7 OVC: 8   TS / CB implies GR   Hill FG implies VIS <200 M

F215

This forecast may be amended at any time.

1. What is the meaning of the following symbol?

    _⋀_

    (a)   Moderate turbulence

    (b)   Moderate icing

    (c)   Severe line squall

    (d)   Freezing rain

2. An aircraft is flying at 4000ft based on QNH 1013hPa in an air mass that has ISA characteristics. If the aircraft flies into an air mass where the temperature is colder than ISA, but QNH is unchanged, what will the aircraft's true altitude be if the altimeter continues to read 4000ft?

    (a)   4000ft

    (b)   Higher than 4000ft

    (c)   FL40

    (d)   Lower than 4000ft

3. Heating of the atmosphere is mostly achieved via:

    (a)   Evaporation of water in the atmosphere

    (b)   Carbon Dioxide emissions

    (c)   Heating of the earth's surface by the sun's radiation

    (d)   Direct heating by the sun's radiation

4. The wind along straight parallel isobars can be referred to as the ....(i).... wind and the wind around curved parallel isobars can be referred to as the ....(ii).... wind:

	(i)	(ii)
(a)	Geostrophic	Gradient
(b)	Pressure	Isobaric
(c)	Cyclonic	Irrigonic
(d)	Coriolis	Friction

5. The conditions most favourable for the formation of radiation fog are:

    (a)   Clear day, low relative humidity, wind 20 knots

    (b)   Clear night, high relative humidity, wind 6 knots

    (c)   Total cloud cover night, low relative humidity, wind 10 knots

    (d)   Clear night, high relative humidity, wind calm

6. You are flying at a constant indicated altitude of 2000ft with a QNH set of 1015hPa. After a long flight with constant starboard drift and without up-dating the pressure setting, a new QNH of 998hPa is passed. Before the updated QNH is applied (ie while 1015 is still set on the altimeter), will the aircraft be:

    (a)   Lower than indicated, the altimeter is over-reading

    (b)   Higher than indicated, the altimeter is under-reading

    (c)   At the altitude shown by the altimeter

    (d)   It depends on the temperature

7. Lenticular clouds are most likely to form in which particular conditions?

   (a) Unstable air with strong convective currents

   (b) Zero wind, air cooled at the surface

   (c) Light winds over oceans

   (d) Stable air rising over a mountain range

8. Which of the following best describes 'water vapour':

   (a) Water droplets held in suspension in the atmosphere and appearing in the form of cloud

   (b) A liquid component of the atmosphere

   (c) A gas present only in the stratosphere

   (d) A gas which makes up a significant proportion of troposphere

9. Polar maritime air reaching the UK is generally:

   (a) Cold, moist, stable

   (b) Cold, dry, unstable

   (c) Warm, moist, stable

   (d) Cold, moist, unstable

10. Which of the following conditions is most likely to cause an aircraft to encounter 'Rain Ice':

    (a) Descending in a cloudless sky from above the freezing level to below the freezing level

    (b) Flight above the freezing level ahead of a warm front in winter

    (c) Flight below the freezing level ahead of a warm front in winter

    (d) Flight in high humidity conditions with an air temperature of +10°C

11. Select which of the following meteorological situations is most likely to lead to carburettor icing:

    (a) Flight above cloud, air temperature −20°C

    (b) Flight close below cloud in rain, air temperature +5°C

    (c) Flight in clear sky, air temperature +30°C

    (d) Flight in clear sky, air temperature −30°C

12. A METAR reads:
    EGSX   160950Z 16005KT 0650E DZ MIFG VV/// 06/05 Q1012 NOSIG=
    Select the correct decode for this METAR:

    (a) Observation timed at 0950 UTC on the 16th; surface wind 160°T 5 knots; minimum visibility 650 metres looking East; moderate Drizzle; Shallow Fog; vertical visibility cannot be assessed; air temperature +6°C, dew point +5°C; QNH1012hPa; No Significant Changes expected in the next two hours

    (b) Observation timed at 0950 UTC on the 16th; surface wind 160°M 5 knots; minimum visibility 650 metres looking East; light Drizzle; Drifting Fog; vertical visibility cannot be assessed; air temperature +6°C, dew point +5°C; QNH1012hPa; No Significant Changes expected this day

    (c) Observation timed at 0950 local on the 16th; surface wind 160°T 5 knots; maximum visibility 650 metres looking East; moderate Drizzle; Shallow Fog; vertical visibility varying; air temperature +6°C, dew point +5°C; QNH1012hPa; No Ground Signals

    (d) Observation timed at 0950 UTC on the 16th; surface wind 160°M 5 knots; minimum visibility 650 metres looking East; light Drizzle; Shallow Fog; vertical visibility cannot be assessed; air temperature +6°C, dew point +5°C; QNH1012hPa; No Signal on ILS

13. Airport A has an elevation of 90ft, Airport B has an elevation of 330ft. The QNH at Airport A is 1014hPa, the QNH at Airport B is 1002hPa. An aircraft is overhead Airport B with that airport's QNH set at an indicated altitude of 2,500ft. If the aircraft flies directly to overhead Airport B, without changing the altimeter pressure setting and maintaining an indicated altitude of 2,500ft, what is it's actual height overhead Airport B? (assume 1hPa = 30ft)

(a)   2530ft

(b)   1810ft

(c)   2500ft

(d)   2140ft

14. A VOLMET broadcast is:

(a)   A recorded broadcast of the METAR for a specific airfield

(b)   A special ATC broadcast, to all aircraft on frequency, of a significant change in weather conditions

(c)   A voluntary met. report

(d)   A recorded broadcast of about 10 METARs for airfields mostly in a specific region

15. In mid-winter conditions an aircraft is flying in a polar maritime air mass. The surface temperature is –5°C, the ISA temperature at 6000ft is:

(a)   -17°C

(b)   +7°C

(c)   +15°C

(d)   +3°C

Turn to the METFORM 214 at appendix A

16. Which of the following most closely represents the forecast wind velocity [i] and temperature [ii] at 5000ft at position 5230N 0230E?

	[i]	[ii]
(a)	170/20	+04°C
(b)	170/20	+7°C
(c)	185/27	+03°C
(d)	190/30	+03°C

Turn to the METFORM 215 at appendix B to answer the following questions

17. The freezing level (where 0°C occurs) at about 54N 0E/W (approximately the centre of the chart) is:

(a)   6000m amsl

(b)   600ft amsl

(c)   6000ft agl

(d)   6000ft amsl

18. The feature identified as [i] on the left-hand side of the forecast chart is:

(a)   A warm front moving at around 7 knots

(b)   An occluding front at around 7 knots

(c)   An occluding front moving at around 12 knots

(d)   A quasi stationary front

19. In Area B 'SURFACE VIS AND WX' the meaning of the term "ISOL 2000M RA/DZ COT FM 10 Z" is:

(a) Isolated above 2000 metres, visibility reduced in rain and/or drizzle, Clear Orographic Turbulence from 10:00 UTC

(b) Isolated 2000m visibility in rain and/or drizzle, on coasts, from 10:00 UTC

(c) Isolated 2000m visibility in rain and/or drizzle, on coasts, from 10:00 LMT

(d) Isolated above 2000 metres, visibility reduced in rain and/or drizzle, Clear Orographic Turbulence from 10000ft

20. Disregard airspace along the stated route for the purposes of answering this question.

A flight is planned from Biggin Hill (A) to Bembridge Isle of White (B) with alternate Southampton (C), routing outside controlled airspace where possible.

The aircraft cannot fly in known icing conditions.

The pilot holds a PPL without instrument qualification, so the flight must be conducted under VFR.

The minimum en-route altitude will be 1000ft agl, the average ground level en-route is 500ft. VMC minima require that the aircraft remains clear of cloud, in sight of the surface and in a minimum flight visibility of 5km.

The estimated time of departure is 1600Z, the time en-route is 1 hour 30 minutes.

The METAR for the departure airfield 'A' at 1550Z is:

26010KT 9999 SCT025 11/3 Q1003

The TAF for the destination airfield 'B' is:

2915/2923 27015KT 9999 SCT025 BECMG 2917/2923 8000 RA BKN009 TEMPO 2919/2923 5000 RA BKN005

Considering this information, and METFORM 215 (appendix B), choose the most reasonable course of action:

(a) Conditions at the airfield 'A' are suitable for departure. Departure should be made as soon as possible to avoid the forecast weather deterioration. The aerodrome forecast for airfield 'B' show the cloud temporarily dropping to 900ft amsl between 1700 and 2300, otherwise conditions in Zone 3 (which covers the whole of the flight) are suitable for VFR flight in all respects

(b) Delaying the departure by two hours will allow the front to clear the area, and the zone 1 conditions behind indicate good visibility and isolated rain showers

(c) The conditions at the departure airfield are generally suitable. However at ETA (1730) at airfield 'B' the aerodrome forecast is for visibility to be falling to 8000m and the cloud base to 900ft. As Zone 2 conditions move to cover the destination there is increased risk of low cloud, rain and reduced visibility. Further, the Zone 3 forecast mentions isolated areas of reduced visibility and low cloud. Cancel the flight.

(d) The departure conditions indicate scattered cloud down to 250ft. Delay the departure until this cloud has cleared. According to the destination aerodrome forecast, conditions there will improve after 1700 so delaying departure will allow arrival into better conditions.

Paper TWO

Appendix A: UK Low-Level Spot Wind Chart (Form 214)

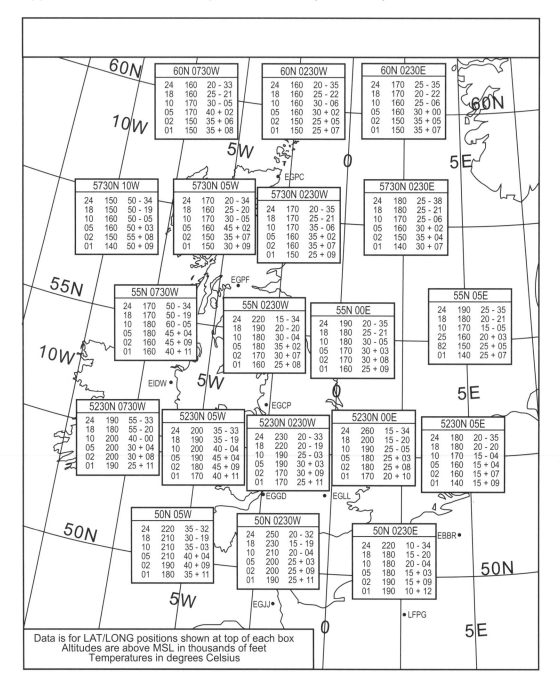

60N 0730W

24	160	20 - 33
18	160	25 - 21
10	170	30 - 05
05	170	40 + 02
02	150	35 + 06
01	150	35 + 08

60N 0230W

24	160	20 - 35
18	160	25 - 22
10	160	30 - 06
05	160	30 + 02
02	150	25 + 05
01	150	25 + 07

60N 0230E

24	170	25 - 35
18	170	20 - 22
10	160	25 - 06
05	160	30 + 00
02	150	35 + 05
01	150	35 + 07

5730N 10W

24	150	50 - 34
18	150	50 - 19
10	160	50 - 05
05	160	50 + 03
02	150	55 + 08
01	140	50 + 09

5730N 05W

24	170	20 - 34
18	160	25 - 20
10	170	30 - 05
05	160	45 + 02
02	150	35 + 07
01	150	30 + 09

5730N 0230W

24	170	20 - 35
18	170	25 - 21
10	170	35 - 06
05	160	35 + 02
02	160	35 + 07
01	150	25 + 09

5730N 0230E

24	180	25 - 38
18	180	25 - 21
10	170	25 - 06
05	160	30 + 02
02	150	35 + 04
01	140	30 + 07

55N 0730W

24	170	50 - 34
18	170	50 - 19
10	180	60 - 05
05	180	45 + 04
02	160	45 + 09
01	160	40 + 11

55N 0230W

24	220	15 - 34
18	190	20 - 20
10	180	30 - 04
05	180	35 + 02
02	170	30 + 07
01	160	25 + 08

55N 00E

24	190	20 - 35
18	180	25 - 21
10	180	30 - 05
05	170	30 + 03
02	170	30 + 08
01	160	25 + 09

55N 05E

24	190	25 - 35
18	180	20 - 21
10	170	15 - 05
25	160	20 + 03
82	150	25 + 05
01	140	25 + 07

5230N 0730W

24	190	55 - 33
18	180	55 - 20
10	200	40 - 00
05	200	30 + 04
02	200	30 + 08
01	190	25 + 11

5230N 05W

24	200	35 - 33
18	190	35 - 19
10	200	40 - 04
05	190	45 + 04
02	180	45 + 09
01	170	40 + 11

5230N 0230W

24	230	20 - 33
18	220	20 - 19
10	190	25 - 03
05	190	30 + 03
02	170	30 + 09
01	170	25 + 11

5230N 00E

24	260	15 - 34
18	200	15 - 20
10	190	25 - 05
05	180	25 + 03
02	180	25 + 08
01	170	20 + 10

5230N 05E

24	180	20 - 35
18	180	20 - 20
10	170	15 - 04
05	160	15 + 04
02	160	15 + 07
01	140	15 + 09

50N 05W

24	220	35 - 32
18	210	30 - 19
10	210	35 - 03
05	210	40 + 04
02	190	40 + 09
01	180	35 + 11

50N 0230W

24	250	20 - 32
18	230	15 - 19
10	210	20 - 04
05	200	25 + 03
02	200	25 + 09
01	190	25 + 11

50N 0230E

24	220	10 - 34
18	180	15 - 20
10	180	20 - 04
05	180	15 + 03
02	190	15 + 09
01	190	10 + 12

Data is for LAT/LONG positions shown at top of each box
Altitudes are above MSL in thousands of feet
Temperatures in degrees Celsius

Appendix B: Forecast Weather (Form 215)

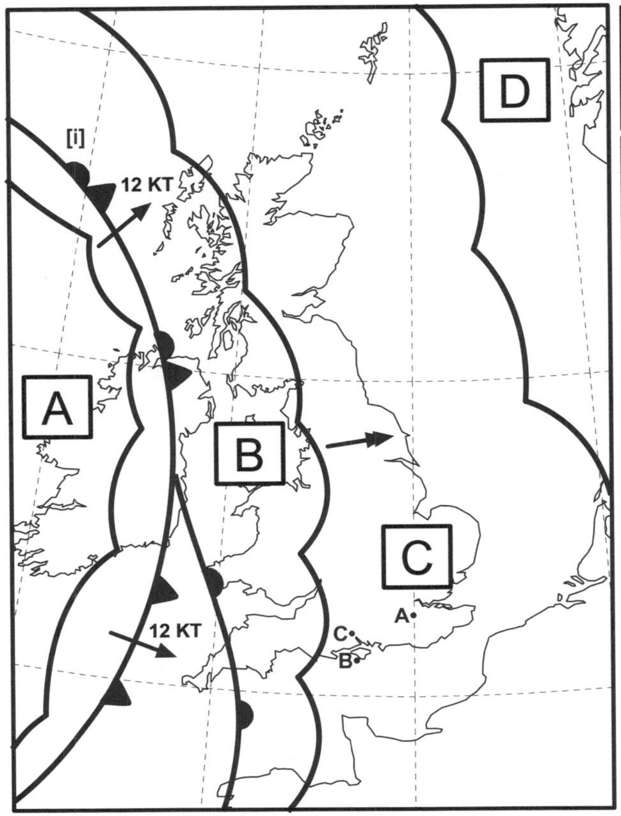

Paper TWO

Forecast Weather

Valid 290800 to 291700 Z   **Fronts/zones valid at 1200 Z**

AREA	SURFACE VIS AND WX	CLOUD	0 C
A	30KM NIL OCNL 8KM SHRA	BKN CU SC 020 - 080 BKN CU SC 015 – XXX	030
B	14KM NIL/RA OCNL 8KM RA ISOL 5000M +RA NEAR FRONT ISOL 2000M RA/DZ COT FM 10 Z	BKN SC 015-060 BKN ST SC 008 – 015 OVC ST005-XXX OVC ST 003-060	070
C	15KM NIL OCNL 6KM NIL ISOL 2500M BR/DZ ISOL 8KM SHRA SW	BKN CU SC 030-060 BKN ST SC 010-070 OVC SC 005 – 070 BKN CU SC 020 – 100	060
D	20KM NIL	FEW SC 025-060	060

Outlook Until:

Similar

All heights in 100's of feet above mean sea level
XXX means above chart upper limit   MOD / SEV ICE   Speed of movement in KT
Cloud amount (Oktas)   MOD / SEV TURB   Temperatures in DEG C
FEW: 1-2   SCT: 3-4   TS / CB implies GR   Hill FG implies VIS <200 M
BKN: 5-7   OVC: 8

This forecast may be amended at any time.

F215

1. Which of the following thunderstorm scenarios is likely to present the greatest hazard to aircraft?

(a)   Dissipating thunderstorms

(b)   Nocturnal thunderstorms

(c)   Well-separated convective thunderstorms in clear air

(d)   Thunderstorms embedded in frontal stratus cloud

2. Although flight near a thunderstorm is not recommended at any time, a thunderstorm is regarded as at its most dangerous to aircraft at low levels:

(a)   During the dissipating stage

(b)   During the onset stage

(c)   During the Cumulus stage

(d)   During its mature stage

3. Which of the following situations is most likely to lead to serious carburettor icing?

(a)   Summer, warm air mass, Descent power

(b)   Summer, warm air mass, Cruise power

(c)   Winter, cold air mass, Descent power

(d)   Winter, cold air mass, Cruise power

4. An aircraft departs from Aerodrome A (elevation 150ft) where the QNH is 997hPa and climbs to an indicated altitude of 3000ft using that pressure setting. The aircraft flies to overhead Aerodrome B (elevation 450ft) where the QNH is 1007hPa. Assume 1 hPa is equivalent to 30ft. If the altimeter subscale setting remains unchanged, and the aircraft remains at an indicated altitude of 3000ft, its actual height over Aerodrome B is:

(a)   2250ft

(b)   2700ft

(c)   3300ft

(d)   2850ft

5. What is the surface wind and meaning of the term 'No Sig' in the following METAR?
EGZZ 231320Z 05005KT 020V080 8000 FEW015 BKN017 02/M01 Q1023 NOSIG

(a)   Surface wind from south east speed five knots. Wind direction variable from 020° to 080° (Magnetic). No significant changes are forecast during the current TAF period.

(b)   Surface wind from north east. Wind direction variable from 020° to 080° (True). No significant changes are forecast during the next 30 minutes.

(c)   Surface wind from the north east, speed five knots. Wind direction variable from 020° to 080° (True). No significant changes are forecast during the two hours after observation time.

(d)   Surface wind from south east, speed five knots. Wind direction variable from 020° to 080° (True). No significant changes are forecast during the four hours after observation time.

6. You are at an airfield (A) where the QNH is 1015hPa, you intend to fly to nearby airfield B which has an elevation of 360ft. Calculate the expected QFE at airfield B (assume that 1hPa = 30ft):

(a)   979hPa

(b)   1015hPa

(c)   1027hPa

(d)   1003hPa

7. Fog that forms just ahead of a warm or occluded front is most likely to be:

(a) Radiation fog

(b) Frontal fog

(c) Steaming Fog

(d) Isobaric fog

8. Which of the following types of icing can occur when flying outside cloud?

(i) carburettor icing

(ii) rain ice

(iii) hoar frost

(iv) rime ice

(v) clear ice

(a) (i), (iii) and (v)

(b) (i), (ii) and (iv)

(c) (iii), (iv) and (v)

(d) (i), (ii) and (iii)

9. In a Tropical Continental air mass in summer over eastern Europe with a surface temperature of +25°C, what is the ISA temperature at 3500ft (rounded to the nearest degree)?

(a) +18°C

(b) +15°C

(c) +8°C

(d) +20°C

10. The force that causes air to start moving from an area of high pressure to an area of low pressure is called:

(a) The Geostrophic force

(b) The Coriolis force

(c) The Pressure Gradient Force

(d) The Isothermic force

11. Which of the following is most likely to occur after several days of a prolonged winter anticyclone in the UK?

(a) Isolated showers with good visibility outside precipitation

(b) Clear, unstable air

(c) Creation of an inversion with cloud and poor visibility beneath

(d) Extensive cumulus or cumulonimbus clouds

12. An aircraft is flying in an air mass whose temperature is colder than ISA at a constant indicated altitude. If the aircraft flies into an air mass which is warmer than ISA, which of the following statements applies:

(a) The aircraft's true altitude will be the same as the indicated altitude if the correct QNH is set

(b) The aircraft's true altitude is likely to be lower than indicated on the altimeter

(c) The aircraft's true altitude is likely to be higher than indicated on the altimeter

(d) The aircraft's true altitude cannot be assessed

13.   What does the following SIGWX chart symbol mean?

   (a)   Severe Turbulence

   (b)   Moderate icing

   (c)   Widespread Fog

   (d)   Hail

14.   An aircraft is flying on a constant track and a constant indicated altitude and is experiencing consistent starboard drift. If the altimeter setting is not updated, which of the following statements is most likely to be correct?

   (a)   The aircraft is flying towards an area of high pressure, the aircraft is higher than the level indicated on the altimeter

   (b)   The aircraft is flying towards an area of low pressure, the aircraft is higher than the level indicated on the altimeter

   (c)   The aircraft is flying towards an area of low pressure, the aircraft is at the level indicated on the altimeter

   (d)   The aircraft is flying towards an area of low pressure, the aircraft is lower than the level indicated on the altimeter

Turn to the METFORM 214 at appendix A

15.   Which of the following most closely represents the forecast wind velocity [i] and temperature [ii] at 5000ft at position 55N 0230E?

	[i]	[ii]
(a)	285/20	+01°C
(b)	270/20	0°C
(c)	285/18	+01°C
(d)	285/10	-01°C

Turn to the METFORM 215 at appendix B to answer the following questions

16.   The freezing level (where 0°C occurs) at about 60N 05W (approximately the top centre of the chart) is:

   (a)   4000m amsl

   (b)   4000ft amsl

   (c)   FL40

   (d)   400m amsl

17.   The weather feature identified as [i] crossing Wales on the forecast chart is:

   (a)   A warm front moving east at around 7 knots

   (b)   A warm front moving west at around 7 knots

   (c)   A warm front moving east at around 15 knots

   (d)   A stationary warm front

18. In zone B, 'CLOUD' section, what is meaning of the following:

"BKN CU SC 020–080" ?

(a)   Broken (5 – 7 oktas) Cumulus and ScatteredCumulus, base 2000ft AGL, tops 8000ft AGL

(b)   Broken (5 – 7 oktas) Cumulus and StratoCumulus, base 2000ft AMSL, tops 8000ft AMSL

(c)   Broken (5 – 7 oktas) Cumulus and StratoCumulus, base 2000ft AGL, tops 8000ft AGL

(d)   Broken (5 – 7 oktas) Cumulus and StratoCumulus, base between 200ft AMSL and 800ft AMSL

19. The outlook on the Metform 215 forecast chart at appendix B can be correctly decoded as:

(a)   Showers along the boundary of Zone A will die out

(b)   Showers in Zone A will die out except at the coast

(c)   Showers, Cloud, Orographic uplift, and Turbulence in Zone A will die out

(d)   Showers in the vicinity of the coast in Zone A will die out

20. Disregard airspace considerations for the purposes of answering this question.

A navigation exercise is planned in the north East Anglia area, routing outside controlled airspace.

The aircraft cannot fly in known icing conditions.

The pilot holds a PPL without instrument qualification, so the flight must be conducted under VFR.

The minimum en-route altitude will be 1000ft agl, the average ground level en-route is 250ft. VMC minima require that the aircraft remains clear of cloud, in sight of the surface and in a minimum flight visibility of 5km.

The estimated time of departure is 1300Z, the exercise will last for around 1 hour 30 minutes. Flight authorisation is based on maintaining an in-flight visibility of not less than 10km.

Considering the METFORM 215 (appendix B), choose the most reasonable course of action:

(a)   Conditions are likely to be no better than 8km visibility in rain, with occasional patches of 5000m in rain/drizzle and cloud base 800ft. Cancel the flight.

(b)   Occasional conditions of 2500m visibility in mist/drizzle and cloud down to 500ft amsl are forecast for the area. Cancel the flight.

(c)   Based on the METFORM 215, conditions are suitable for the planned flight and it should be able to proceed as planned.

(d)   The departure should be delayed to allow conditions to improve as zone 3 moves into the region after 1700Z.

Paper THREE

Appendix A: UK Low-Level Spot Wind Chart (Form 214)

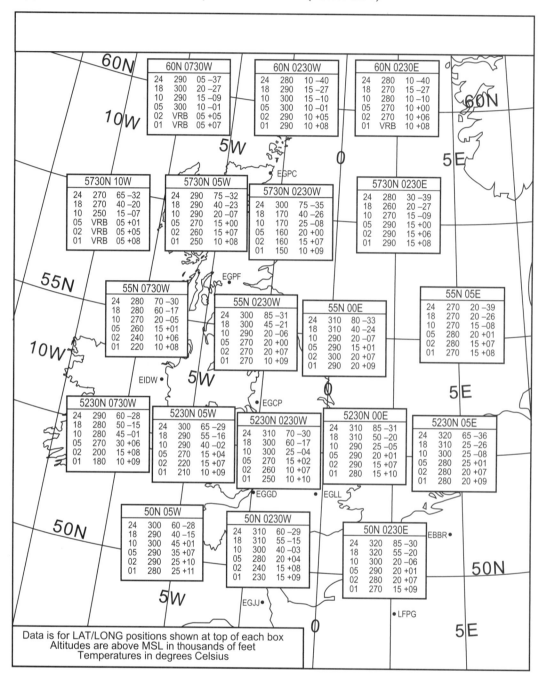

60N 0730W		
24	290	05 −37
18	300	20 −27
10	290	15 −09
05	300	10 −01
02	VRB	05 +05
01	VRB	05 +07

60N 0230W		
24	280	10 −40
18	290	15 −27
10	300	15 −10
05	300	10 −01
02	290	10 +05
01	290	10 +08

60N 0230E		
24	280	10 −40
18	270	15 −27
10	280	10 −10
05	270	10 +00
02	270	10 +06
01	VRB	10 +08

5730N 10W		
24	270	65 −32
18	270	40 −20
10	250	15 −07
05	VRB	05 +01
02	VRB	05 +05
01	VRB	05 +08

5730N 05W		
24	290	75 −32
18	290	40 −23
10	290	20 −07
05	270	15 +00
02	260	15 +07
01	250	10 +08

5730N 0230W		
24	300	75 −35
18	170	40 −26
10	170	25 −08
05	160	20 +00
02	160	15 +07
01	150	10 +09

5730N 0230E		
24	280	30 −39
18	260	20 −27
10	270	15 −09
05	290	15 +00
02	290	15 +06
01	290	15 +08

EGPC

55N 0730W		
24	280	70 −30
18	280	60 −17
10	270	20 −05
05	260	15 +01
02	240	10 +06
01	220	10 +08

55N 0230W		
24	300	85 −31
18	300	45 −21
10	290	20 −06
05	270	20 +00
02	270	20 +07
01	270	10 +09

55N 00E		
24	310	80 −33
18	310	40 −24
10	290	20 −07
05	290	15 +01
02	300	20 +07
01	290	20 +09

55N 05E		
24	270	20 −39
18	270	20 −26
10	270	15 −08
05	280	20 +01
02	280	15 +07
01	270	15 +08

EGPF

5230N 0730W		
24	290	60 −28
18	280	50 −15
10	280	45 −01
05	270	30 +06
02	200	15 +08
01	180	10 +09

5230N 05W		
24	300	65 −29
18	290	55 −16
10	290	40 −02
05	270	15 +04
02	220	15 +07
01	210	10 +09

5230N 0230W		
24	310	70 −30
18	300	60 −17
10	300	25 −04
05	270	15 +02
02	260	10 +07
01	250	10 +10

5230N 00E		
24	310	85 −31
18	310	50 −20
10	290	25 −05
05	290	20 +01
02	290	15 +07
01	280	15 +10

5230N 05E		
24	320	65 −36
18	310	25 −26
10	300	25 −08
05	280	25 +01
02	280	20 +07
01	280	20 +09

EIDW
EGCP
EGGD
EGLL

50N 05W		
24	300	60 −28
18	290	40 −15
10	300	45 +01
05	290	35 +07
02	290	25 +10
01	280	25 +11

50N 0230W		
24	310	60 −29
18	310	55 −15
10	300	40 −03
05	280	20 +04
02	240	15 +08
01	230	15 +09

50N 0230E		
24	320	85 −30
18	320	55 −20
10	300	20 −06
05	290	20 +01
02	280	20 +07
01	270	15 +09

EBBR
EGJJ
LFPG

Data is for LAT/LONG positions shown at top of each box
Altitudes are above MSL in thousands of feet
Temperatures in degrees Celsius

Appendix B: Forecast Weather (Form 215)

Forecast Weather

Valid 211400 to 212300 Z   **Fronts/zones valid at**   **1800Z**

AREA	SURFACE VIS AND WX	CLOUD	0 C
A	25KM NIL OCNL 2500M BR/DZ SEA/COT ISOL 10KM SHRA LAND ISOL 7KM SHRA LAND N	BKN CU SC 025 – 060 BKN ST 005 – 015 BKN CU SC 020 – 080 BKN CU AC 016 – XXX ∇ ⌄	040 – 060
B	8KM RA OCNL 5000M RA/RADZ ISOL 500M FG DZ W OF FRONT ISOL 15KM NIL	BKN SC 020-070 BKN ST SC 008 – 070 OVC 000-5000 FEW/BKN SC 020-050	070 – 100
C	12KM NIL OCNL 5000M BR/RADZ OCNL 20KM NIL MAINLY SW	SCT/BKN ST SC 010-050 BKN ST SC 005-060 SCT/BKN SC 015 – 050	100

Outlook Until:

Showers COT Zone A dying out

All heights in 100's of feet above mean sea level
XXX means above chart upper limit   Speed of movement in KT
Cloud amount (Oktas)   MOD / SEV ICE   Temperatures in DEG C
FEW : 1-2   SCT: 3-4   MOD / SEV TURB   Hill FG implies VIS <200 M
BKN: 5-7   OVC: 8   TS / CB implies GR

This forecast may be amended at any time.

F215

Meteorology paper 1 Q1   Answer D

'Rotor' is an area of exceptionally dangerous turbulence that can form just downwind of a ridge when a strong wind is blowing across it. Rotor is occasionally marked by an area of 'roll' or 'rotor' cloud.

Further reference: PPL3 > Meteorology > Flight over Mountainous Areas and Other Weather Hazards > Mountain Waves

Meteorology paper 1 Q2   Answer B

Relative humidity is the percentage of water vapour a parcel of air is holding, compared to the amount it could hold before becoming saturated. A parcel of air containing half the water vapour it could hold before becoming saturated has a relative humidity (RH) of 50%. A relative humidity of 100% means that the air is saturated, it is holding all the water vapour it can before condensation will occur and visible water droplets (eg cloud) form.

As the temperature of air decreases it is able to hold less water vapour before becoming saturated. So, even though its water content may remain the same, as air is cooled its relative humidity will increase until, at the dew point temperature, it reaches saturation.

Further Reference: PPL3 > Meteorology > Humidity and Stability > Humidity

Meteorology paper 1 Q3   Answer D

Over the land, surface friction means that typically the 2000ft wind is slowed by around 50% and backed by up to 30° at the surface. A 'backing' in direction means that the direction as expressed in degrees reduces (move backwards). Given a 2000ft wind of 240/35, the closest fit to this modification is answer D, with reduction in speed of a backing about 40% and a backing in direction of 20°.

Further reference: PPL3 > Meteorology > The Motion of the Atmosphere > Variation of Wind Velocity with Altitude

Meteorology paper 1 Q4   Answer C

The wind blowing over a mountain range can create large scale disturbances in the atmosphere. These disturbances are usually referred to as mountain waves. Mountains cause the air flow to undulate, like waves in the ocean. Where mountain waves rise up (also known as orographic uplift), gliders have reached great heights with their assistance.

However, where the waves turn down they can force aircraft to descend, even at full power and best climb airspeed. This can continue right down to ground level.

When cloud forms in a mountain wave, it will often be of the "lenticular" variety. This is smooth and elongated cloud – not unlike an almond in appearance – and actually remains stationary at the 'crest' of the wave, the cloud forming at the leading edge and dissipating at the trailing edge. In favourable conditions for orographic uplift there may be lenticular clouds at the crest of each wave, and even several such clouds piled on top of one another.

Further reference: PPL3 > Meteorology > Flight over Mountainous Areas and Other Weather Hazards > Mountain Waves

Meteorology paper 1 Q5   Answer A

Airflow around a depression (an area of low pressure) in the Northern Hemisphere flows anti-clockwise. It follows that an aircraft flying directly towards the centre of a depression will experience a wind which will cause it to drift to the right (starboard).

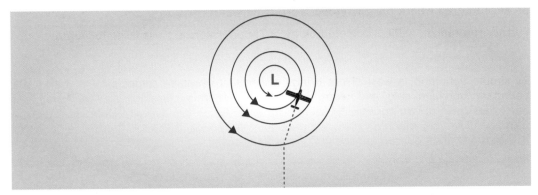

Further reference: PPL3 > Meteorology > The Motion of the Atmosphere > Depressions and Anticyclones

Meteorology paper 1 Q6   Answer A

In the International Standard Atmosphere (ISA), the surface temperature is +15°C, decreasing at a rate of 1.98°C (shall we call it 2°C?) per 1000ft as altitude increases.

Thus, at 7,000ft in the ISA, the reduction in temperature from the surface is (7 x 2°C = 14°C), 15°C – 14°C = +1°C

Further reference: PPL3 > Meteorology > The International Standard Atmosphere > The Parameters of the ISA

Meteorology paper 1 Q7   Answer D

The theoretical diurnal (daily) variation in temperature can be affected by many 'real world' variations. Nevertheless, in theory if there is no cloud cover, local winds or change of air mass, overnight the surface temperature falls as heat radiates out into space. This process continues until the incoming radiation from the sun begins to reverse the process but there is a lag in this feeding through to the surface temperature. Therefore the theoretical coldest temperature at the surface occurs just after sunrise (dawn).

Further reference: PPL3 > Meteorology > The Motion of the Atmosphere > Local Winds

Meteorology paper 1 Q8   Answer C

The troposphere is the layer of atmosphere in contact with the surface, and this is where virtually all 'weather' occurs. The troposphere is capped by an effective 'lid' on the weather in the form of a temperature inversion known as the tropopause. The level of the tropopause varies from around 20,000ft over the poles to 60,000ft over the tropics. Above the tropopause, the thin, dry and cold air of the stratosphere makes any weather (eg clouds and precipitation) quite rare.

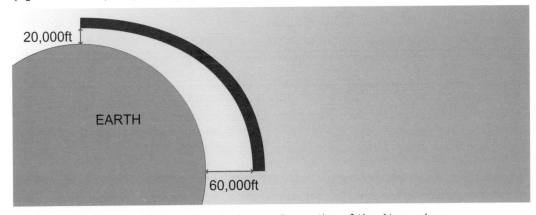

Further reference: PPL3 > Meteorology > Properties of the Atmosphere > Composition and Structure

Answers ONE

Meteorology paper 1 Q9   Answer A

The general advice to pilots is that airframe icing can be expected anywhere within a thunderstorm cloud.

Nevertheless, in accordance with normal icing theory, the most severe icing is likely to be encountered where the air temperature is between 0°c and –30°c.

Further reference: PPL3 > Meteorology > Thunderstorms > Hazards for Aircraft

Meteorology paper 1 Q10   Answer B

By simple definition, a warm front brings warm air to replace colder air – it marks the boundary between cold and warm air masses. By this classification, the choice is narrowed down to two possible answers. The assumption the average slope of a 'typical' warm front is very much an idealised theoretical principle, although the figure of 1:150 is that most often quoted in meteorological textbooks.

Further reference: PPL3 > Meteorology > Low Pressure Systems – Depressions > Definition of a Front & The Warm Front

Meteorology paper 1 Q11   Answer C

Flying ahead of a warm front in winter is a 'classic' situation in which to encounter rain ice – potentially a very hazardous situation.

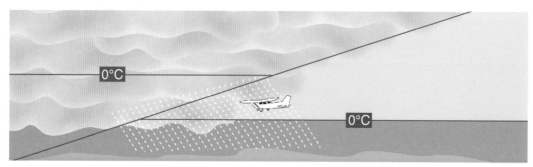

As the air temperature is –2°C (ie below freezing), it is safe to assume that the surface of the aircraft itself (especially a metal surface) will also be below freezing. Precipitation falling as liquid rain through the warm front (possible because of the higher freezing level in the warm air behind the warm front) can freeze on contact with the cold aircraft skin, leading to small lumps of ice forming all over the upper surfaces of the aircraft which are very difficult to remove. The weight and drag caused by this rain ice has very serious implications for the performance and handling characteristics of the afflicted aircraft.

Further reference: PPL3 > Meteorology > Icing > Rain Ice

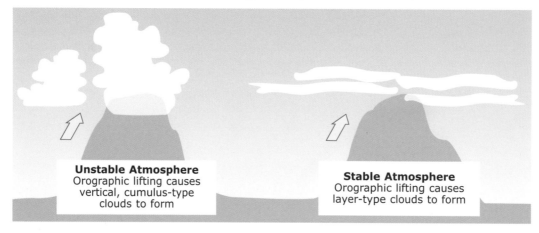

Unstable Atmosphere
Orographic lifting causes vertical, cumulus-type clouds to form

Stable Atmosphere
Orographic lifting causes layer-type clouds to form

Meteorology paper 1 Q12   Answer D

The key word in the question is that referring to an 'unstable' air mass. If unstable air is forced to rise (in this case by a mountain range – orographic lifting), the result is most often cloud of mostly vertical extent – namely cumulus-type or 'Cumuloform' clouds.

Further reference: PPL3 > Meteorology > Clouds and Precipitation > Formation of Clouds

Meteorology paper 1 Q13   Answer C

To answer this question, you first need to know what types of cloud the abbreviations are referring to. In summary, the cloud-type abbreviations are:

High Level Cloud	CI	Cirrus
	CS	Cirrostratus
	CC	Cirrocumulus
Medium Level Cloud	AS	Altostratus
	AC	Altocumulus
Low Level Cloud	ST	Stratus
	CU	Cumulus
	SC	Stratocumulus
	NS	Nimbostratus
Cloud that may exist through all levels	CB	Cumulonimbus
	TCU	Towering Cumulus

Next you need to know that a 'typical' warm front (a situation found more in text books than in real-life), brings with it mostly layered type clouds, starting with high-level Cirrus (CI) at the top of the warm front slope, gradually thickening – Cirrostratus (CS), and descending – Altostratus (AS), as the front approaches with low Stratus (ST) and Nimbostratus (NS) at the passage of the front.

Answer D is the only sequence that describes this idealised 'typical' warm front cloud progression.

Further reference: PPL3 > Meteorology > Low Pressure Systems – Depressions > The Warm Front

Meteorology paper 1 Q14   Answer A

The four main air masses that affect the UK can be broadly characterised as follows:

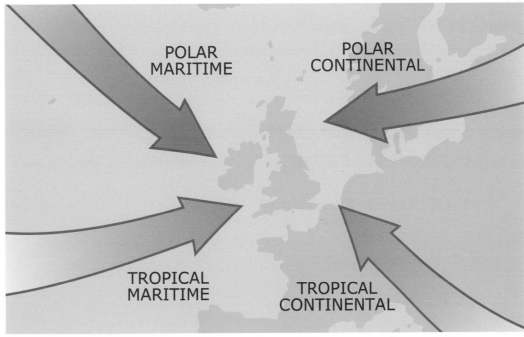

Air Mass	Stability	Visibility	Cloud Types
Tropical Martime	Stable	Poor	Extensive stratus-type
Tropical Continental	Stable	Becoming Poor	Little cloud
Polar Continental	Stable	Good	Little cloud
Polar Maritime	Unstable	Good	Frequent showers

Further reference: PPL3 > Meteorology > Air Masses > Characteristics of Air Masses

Meteorology paper 1 Q15   Answer B

At the position given (50N 00E/W) there is no data box. Therefore it is necessary to interpolate between the closest data boxes – namely those at 50N 0230W and 50N 0230E. It happens that the position given is half-way between each box.

The 2000ft wind at 50N 0230W is 280° at 15 knots, at 50N 0230E it is 260° at 20 knots.

To interpolate mathematically between these figures, they can beaded together and divided by two;

i.e.

260 + 280 ÷2 = **270** (although it is clear even without a formulae that 270 is half way between 260 and 280).

In the same way;

15 + 20 ÷2 = 17·5, which is rounded up to **18**,

The temperature is interpolated in the same way:

11 + 14 ÷2 = 12·5, which is rounded up to **+13**

Remember, if your calculation gives a slightly different answer to any of the given options, you should select the one which is closest to your answer.

Further reference: PPL3 > Meteorology > Aviation Weather Reports and Forecasts > Specific Forecast and Actual Formats

Meteorology paper 1 Q16   Answer A

The 0°C isotherm (in other words, the freezing level) is given as a figure representing thousands of feet above mean sea level (amsl) – see the text explanation on the left-hand side of the charts.

Further reference: PPL3 > Meteorology > Aviation Weather Reports and Forecasts > Specific Forecast and Actual Formats

Meteorology paper 1 Q17   Answer C

"ISOL" = Isolated

"4000M" = 4000 metres visibility

"+SHRA" = heavy shower of rain

"+TSGR" = heavy thunderstorm with hail

"MON" = Mountain

"N 56N" = North of latitude 56°N

Further reference: PPL3 > Meteorology > Aviation Weather Reports and Forecasts > Specific Forecast and Actual Formats

Meteorology paper 1 Q18   Answer B

For a full list of met. symbols, see the essential revision section.

Further reference: PPL3 > Meteorology > Aviation Weather Reports and Forecasts > Specific Forecast and Actual Formats

Meteorology paper 1 Q19   Answer C

"BKN" = Broken (5-7 oktas) cloud cover

"CB" = Cumulonimbus cloud type

"008" = 800ft above mean sea level (amsl)

"XXX" = Above chart upper limit

        = Severe icing

        = Severe turbulence

Further reference: PPL3 > Meteorology > Aviation Weather Reports and Forecasts >
Specific Forecast and Actual Formats

Meteorology paper 1 Q20   Answer C

Consideration of the departure METAR, arrival TAF and Zone 2 condition on the METFORM 215 give a view of generally good in-flight visibility, with a cloud base at around 2500amsl. There may be showers en-route, and these also may occur temporarily at the destination airfield, but only after 1600 (ie about the arrival ETA). In the good visibility, it should be possible to see and avoid and showers to good time. It is reasonable to proceed with the planned flight, exercising caution to avoid any showers.

All the other answer options are based on a mis-reading of the METAR, TAF or METFORM215 information.

Further reference: PPL3 > Meteorology > Aviation Weather Reports and Forecasts >
Specific Forecast and Actual Formats

Meteorology paper 2 Q1   Answer A

The most common significant weather symbols used on (SIGWX) charts are found in the essential revision section: they should be learnt.

Further reference: PPL3 > Meteorology > Aviation Weather Reports and Forecasts > Specific Forecast and Actual Formats

Meteorology paper 2 Q2   Answer D

The key element of the question is that the aircraft has moved from an air mass with an ISA temperature structure to an air mass which is colder than ISA. In air which is colder (and so more dense) than ISA, the altimeter will indicate that the aircraft is higher than it really is, even if the pressure setting is correct. For precision flight in extremely cold conditions, it may be necessary to correct indicated altitude for this 'temperature' error using special tables.

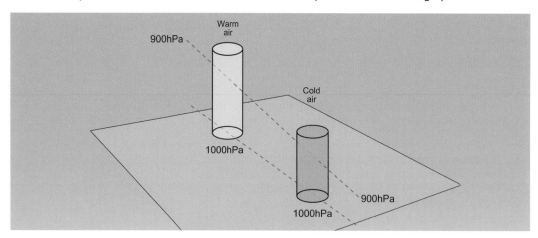

Further reference: PPL3 > Meteorology > Pressure and Altimetry > Altimetry

Meteorology paper 2 Q3   Answer C

The atmosphere itself acquires virtually no heat energy directly from the sun – it is essentially transparent to solar radiation. Radiation from the sun heats up the earth's surface, and the atmosphere is then warmed from below. In effect, the sun's energy (heat) only heats the atmosphere by re-radiation from the surface. The differing surfaces of the earth (land, sea, snow cover etc.), the shape of the earth and the fact that the earth is tilted on its axis means that surface heating is not uniform across the globe, leading to the movement of air around the planet.

Further reference: PPL3 > Meteorology > The Motion of the Atmosphere > Heating of the Atmosphere

Meteorology paper 2 Q4   Answer A

Air first begins to move under the influence of pressure gradient force – air moves form high pressure towards low pressure. Once air is in motion, it is acted upon by the Coriolis force which deflects air to the right in the northern hemisphere (and to the left in the southern hemisphere).

At some point, a balance will be reached between the effect of the pressure gradient force and the Coriolis force. Where the resulting balanced wind is following straight, parallel isobars, the resulting wind is sometimes referred to as the Geostrophic wind. When the balanced wind is following curved isobars it can be referred to as the gradient wind. This second definition takes into account the effect of centrifugal force in addition to the pressure gradient force and Coriolis force that define the Geostrophic wind.

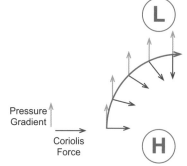

Further reference: PPL3 > Meteorology > The Motion of the Atmosphere > Coriolis Force, Geostrophic Wind

Meteorology paper 2 Q5   Answer B

The classic factors in the formation of radiation fog are:

- A night with little or no cloud cover allowing cooling of the surface by radiation
- High relative humidity
- Light winds, say 2-8 knots

These criteria do not absolutely guarantee that radiation fog will form. These conditions can occur and no fog form; alternatively radiation fog can form in slightly different conditions. Nevertheless, these criteria represent a good guide to conditions most likely to lead to radiation fog.

Further reference: PPL3 > Meteorology > Visibility > Fog and Mist

Meteorology paper 2 Q6   Answer A

Firstly:

Starboard = Right

Port = Left

One way of remembering this is that 'Port' and 'Left' have the same number of letters. Not very catchy, but it is true.

The fact that the aircraft is flying with a constant starboard drift indicates that the wind is blowing from the left. According to Buys Ballot's law, in the northern hemisphere if you stand with your back to the wind, the low pressure area is on your left. Transposed onto the situation in the question, this indicates that the aircraft is flying towards an area of low pressure.

This presumption is confirmed by the fact that when the altimeter pressure setting is updated, the new QNH is lower than before.

If an aircraft flies towards a low pressure area without updating the sub-scale setting, the altimeter will **over-read** – the aircraft is lower than the altimeter reading.

Hence the saying; "**high to low, down you go**".

Although the question does not ask for the exact magnitude of the error, based on 1hPa = 30ft you can calculate that before changing setting the altimeter was over-reading by 510ft (ie the hPa difference of 17hPa x 30ft). Therefore the altimeter was indicating that the aircraft was 510ft higher than it really was: the indicated altitude of 2000ft equates to an actual altitude of 1490ft (2000ft – 510ft).

Further reference: PPL3 > Meteorology > The Motion of the Atmosphere >
Depressions and Anticyclones
and
PPL3 > Meteorology > Pressure and Altimetry > Altimetry

Answers TWO

Meteorology paper 2 Q7   Answer D

When air is forced to rise by terrain (such as a mountain or mountain range) it can be said to be undergoing 'orographic lifting', and where stable air flows over a mountain or a range of mountains, particularly in strong wind conditions, this lifting action can lead to the formation of mountain waves, also known as 'standing waves' or 'lee waves'. These waves are sought out by glider pilots who can use the orographic uplift to reach spectacular altitudes, although the downdraughts where the waves turn down can be equally spectacular in the opposite sense.

Lenticular clouds are stationary saucer-shaped clouds that sometimes form at the crests of these waves. Due to their shape, lack of movement and exceptionally smooth contours lenticular clouds have been mistaken for UFOs in the past! To a meteorologist, lenticular clouds belong to the 'lenticularis species' (clouds formed in the lee wave parallel to a mountain ridge) and can be classified by meteorologists as altocumulus lenticularis, stratocumulus lenticularis or cirrocumulus lenticularis.

Further reference: PPL3 > Meteorology > Flight Over Mountainous Areas and Other Weather Hazards > Mountain Waves

Meteorology paper 2 Q8   Answer D

Water vapour is a gas, put simply it is water in its gas state and as such it is invisible. Water in the atmosphere only becomes visible when water vapour changes state either by condensing into liquid water droplets (eg cloud, fog, steam) or sublimating into solid water – ice – (eg frost). Virtually all water vapour is found in the troposphere (the lowest level of the atmosphere) and it is responsible for the formation of clouds, fog, precipitation etc.

The proportion of water vapour in the troposphere varies but it is generally considered to be the third largest component of the lower atmosphere after nitrogen and oxygen.

Further reference: PPL3 Meteorology > Properties of the Atmosphere > Composition and Structure

Meteorology paper 2 Q9   Answer D

The fact that the air is coming from a polar region, and that it is a maritime airflow, indicates that it is cold and moist. Because the air is being warmed from beneath as it travels southwards, it tends to become unstable – as a rule air masses become unstable if heat energy is put into them.

Further reference: PPL3 > Meteorology > Air Masses > Characteristics of Air Masses

Meteorology paper 2 Q10   Answer B

The 'classic' situation for rain ice to occur is ahead of a warm front in winter. Rain falls from the warm air of the warm front into the cold air ahead of it. If this rain hits an object with a surface temperature that is below freezing (for example, an aircraft flying above the freezing level), it is likely that the rain will freeze into it instantly, causing 'rain' or 'clear' ice to form.

Such ice is very difficult to remove and hence very dangerous.

Further reference: PPL3 > Meteorology > Icing > Rain Ice

Meteorology paper 2 Q11   Answer B

The dominant factor in carburettor icing is humidity – the more humid the air, the more likely carburettor icing. The temperature fall within the carburettor can be as much as 25°C, so temperatures below freezing, or above +30°C make carburettor icing far less likely. Of the options listed, the flight near cloud, in rain is clearly the most humid situation, with an air temperature (+5°C) which is within the range where carburettor icing can be considered likely.

Further reference: PPL3 > Meteorology > Icing > Piston Engine Icing

Meteorology paper 2 Q12   Answer A

The full METAR and TAF decode must be learnt. Some further key points to remember:

All times are in UTC

Wind directions in a METAR report are in ° True unless otherwise specified.

The direction of the minimum visibility is only given if there is a significant variation in visibility when looking in different directions.

The symbol '//' is used to denote missing information

Further reference: PPL3 > Meteorology > Aviation Weather Reports and Forecasts > Specific Forecast and Actual Formats

Meteorology paper 2 Q13   Answer B

The aircraft has flown towards an area of lower pressure without re-setting its altimeter pressure setting, therefore even with the same indicated altitude, it is actually lower than indicated ("High to low, down you go"). The difference in altimeter pressure setting is 12hPa (1014 – 1002); 12 x 30ft = 360ft difference. Hence, at an indicated altitude of 2,500ft, when the aircraft is overhead Airfield B its actual <u>altitude</u> is 2,500 – 360 = 2140ft.

However, the question requires the aircraft's <u>height</u> above Airfield B. If airfield B has an elevation (its height above sea level) of 330ft, the height of the aircraft when overhead Airfield B is 2140ft – 330ft = 1810ft.

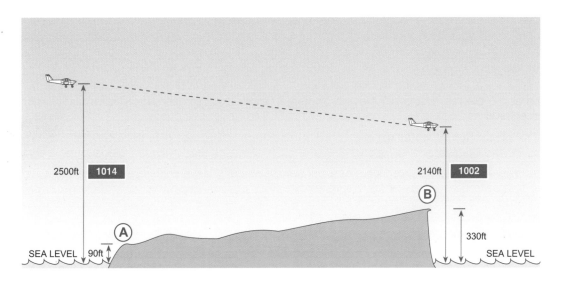

Further reference: PPL3 > Meteorology > Pressure and Altimetry > Altimetry

Answers TWO

Meteorology paper 2 Q14   Answer D

A VOLMET service is an automatic broadcast of recorded METARs for a number of airfields (usually around 10-12), grouped mostly in the same area. The name of the VOLMET broadcast will normally be the FIR name, plus a more precise region – e.g. 'London Volmet North', 'Paris Volmet' etc. Full details of VOLMET broadcasts including frequency, airfields covered etc. will be found in the appropriate AIPs and also commercial flight guides.

Further reference: PPL3 > Meteorology > Aviation Weather Reports and Forecasts > Obtaining Met. Information In-Flight

Meteorology paper 2 Q15   Answer D

The air temperature at various levels in the International Standard Atmosphere (ISA) is fixed and does not vary with season, location or air mass (this is the point of ISA after all).

In the ISA the surface is +15°C, the temperature reduces at 2°C per 1000ft as altitude increases. Therefore at 6000ft, the ISA temperature is 15 – (6x2), = +3°C

Further reference: PPL3 > Meteorology > The International Standard Atmosphere > The Parameters of the ISA

Meteorology paper 2 Q16   Answer A

At the position given (5230N 0230E) there is no data box. Check that again – the position given is 0230 EAST not 0230 WEST. Because there is no data box at the position given it is necessary to interpolate between the closest data boxes – namely those at 5230N 00E and 5230N 05E. The position given is half-way between each box.

The 5000ft wind at 5230N 00E is 180° at 25 knots, at 5230N 05E it is 160° at 15 knots.

Interpolating between these figures is fairly simple, giving a mid-point of 170° at 20 knots

The temperature is interpolated in the same way, and rounded up to +4°C

Remember, if your calculation gives a slightly different answer to any of the answer options, you should select the option which is closest to your calculation.

Further reference: PPL3 > Meteorology > Aviation Weather Reports and Forecasts > Specific Forecast and Actual Formats

Meteorology paper 2 Q17   Answer D

The 0°C isotherm (in other words, the freezing level) is given as a figure representing thousands of feet above mean sea level (amsl) – see the text explanation on the left-hand side of the charts.

Further reference: PPL3 > Meteorology > Aviation Weather Reports and Forecasts > Specific Forecast and Actual Formats

Meteorology paper 2 Q18   Answer C

For a full list of met. symbols, see the essential revision section. The speed of movement of the front is given on the 'arrow' that crosses the front.

Further reference: PPL3 > Meteorology > Aviation Weather Reports and Forecasts > Specific Forecast and Actual Formats

Meteorology paper 2 Q19   Answer B

ISOL = Isolated

2000M = 2000m visibility

RA/DZ = rain and/or drizzle

COT = Coast

FM 10 Z = from 10:00 Zulu (UTC)

Further reference: PPL3 > Meteorology > Aviation Weather Reports and Forecasts > Specific Forecast and Actual Formats

Meteorology paper 2 Q20   Answer C

Consideration of the departure METAR, arrival TAF and Zone 3 conditions on the METFORM 215 give a view of generally deteriorating weather situation, with the aircraft flying almost directly into the worsening weather of the occluding front. The conditions of Zone 2 (the occluding front) will begin to arrive at the destination around the ETA. Moreover, even in Zone 3 areas of mist and drizzle, with visibility down to 2500m and cloud base effectively down to ground level, are forecast. This combination of marginal en-route weather and the forecast deterioration at the destination make safe VFR flight unlikely.

All the other answer options are based on a misreading of the METAR, TAF or METFORM215 information, or a failure to appreciate that Zone 2 conditions will move to cover the destination airfield.

Further reference: PPL3 > Meteorology > Aviation Weather Reports and Forecasts > Specific Forecast and Actual Formats

Meteorology paper 3 Q1   Answer D

All thunderstorms are hazardous to aircraft, and the universal advice is that all aircraft and pilots should avoid all thunderstorms.

Where thunderstorms occur in clear conditions and are well-separated, avoidance is not usually a problem – they are easy to see and avoid. At night, the lightning from an active thunderstorm may be visible from hundreds of miles away to an aircraft in flight – again avoidance should not be a problem in these circumstances.

Conversely, thunderstorms that are embedded inside extensive cloud – for example the layered cloud of a warm or occluded front – present a particular hazard precisely because they cannot be seen: they are masked by the frontal cloud. Thus it is possible for a pilot flying in cloud to blunder straight into a thunderstorm that could have easily been avoided if it was in clear air. Many pilots regard embedded thunderstorms as one of the greatest aviation weather hazards.

Further reference: PPL3 > Meteorology > Thunderstorms > Practical Advice for Thunderstorm Avoidance

Meteorology paper 3 Q2   Answer D

Thunderstorms are generally considered to have a three-stage life-cycle:

■ the 'Cumulus stage' as the thunderstorm first begins to grow vertically taller than a 'normal' Cumulus cloud;

■ the 'Mature stage' when precipitation first begins to fall from the storm – it is at this stage that vertical currents are at their most intense and so hazards such as turbulence and windshear are at their strongest;

■ the 'Dissipating stage' as the storm begins to subside, although it remains dangerous to aircraft.

A thunderstorm is at its most active during the 'mature' stage and so this is when it represents the greatest hazard, but it must be appreciated that a thunderstorm is dangerous to some extent throughout the whole of its lifecycle. There is no such thing as a safe thunderstorm.

Further reference: PPL3 > Meteorology > Thunderstorms > The Formation and Life-Cycle of Thunderstorms

Meteorology paper 3 Q3   Answer A

Contrary to what might seem common sense, carburettor icing is probably more likely to occur in summer – for the simple reason that warm air can hold more moisture (which in turn is converted into more ice) than cold air. The higher the moisture content of the air, the more likely carburettor icing.

The temperature drop within the carburettor can be anything up to 25°C, so even on at hot summer day (air temperature say +25°C), the air inside the carburettor venturi may be below freezing. Ironically during the winter (air temperature say 0°C), the further temperature drop within the carburettor means that any moisture in the air tends to turn into ice crystals which pass through the carburettor rather than sticking and blocking it.

Under any set of conditions, a low power setting (such as that used during a descent) makes carburettor icing more likely.

Further reference: PPL3 > Meteorology > Icing > Piston Engine Icing

Meteorology paper 3 Q4   Answer D

Because the aircraft is flying from low pressure to high pressure without changing its altimeter subscale setting, it will be higher than indicated on the altimeter. The pressure difference between airfield A and airfield B is 10hPa, which equates to a vertical distance of 300ft (10hPa x 30ft). Thus, when overhead Airfield B at an indicated altitude of 3000ft, the aircraft is actually at an altitude (amsl) of 3300ft.

However, the question asks for the aircraft's height above airfield B. If Airfield B has an elevation (its vertical distance above sea level) of 450ft, an aircraft at an altitude of 3300ft is at a height of 2850ft over Airfield B (3300ft – 450ft).

Further reference: PPL3 > Meteorology > Pressure and Altimetry > Altimetry

Meteorology paper 3 Q5   Answer C

The TAF and METAR decodes are used worldwide and need to be learnt thoroughly – not just for exam purposes.

Note that the correct definition of NO SIG when used in a METAR is that **NO SIG**nificant changes are forecast to occur during the trend forecast period. The trend forecast period is the two hours after the observation time.

Further reference: PPL3 > Meteorology > Aviation Weather Reports and Forecasts >
                       Specific Forecast and Actual Formats

Meteorology paper 3 Q6   Answer D

This problem is best solved in stages.

QNH is the altimeter pressure setting which indicates the vertical distance above sea level. QFE is the altimeter pressure setting which indicates vertical distance above a fixed point (such as an airfield).

Because airfields are normally above sea level, it is usually the case that an airfield QFE will be a lower value than an airfield QNH.

The difference between QNH and QFE is the airfield elevation (QNH and QFE can only be the same if the airfield is at sea level). In this case airfield B has an elevation – its vertical distance above sea level – of 360ft.

The question tells you to assume that 1hPa = 30ft. Therefore, the difference in pressure over 360ft is 360 ÷ 30 = 12hPa.

QFE will be less than QNH, so QNH (1015hPa) minus 12hPa gives an anticipated QFE at airfield B of 1015 – 12 = 1003hPa.

Further reference: PPL3 > Meteorology > Pressure and Altimetry > Altimetry

Meteorology paper 3 Q7   Answer B

Frontal fog occasionally forms just ahead of a warm or occluded front as the surface air becomes saturated by continuous rain. Rain falling from warm air above the front evaporates at or near the surface in the colder air ahead of the front. This cools the air whilst adding to the air's moisture content until the air becomes saturated and condensation (visible water droplets) occurs. Frontal fog (sometimes called precipitation fog) is most common in the vicinity of a slow moving or stationary warm or occluded front, the key factors include light winds and continuous precipitation.

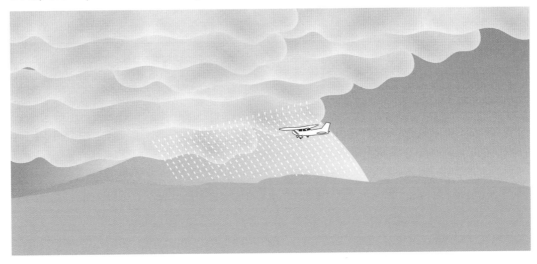

Further reference: PPL3 > Meteorology > Visibility > Fog and Mist

Meteorology paper 3 Q8.   Answer D

The main types of icing can be summarised as follows:

Type of Ice	Characteristics
Carburettor icing	Icing inside the carburettor caused by the temperature drop within the venturi, can occur in clear air conditions
Rain ice	Rare form of icing that can occur ahead of a warm front in winter. Liquid precipitation falls into colder air and freezes on contact with a surface below freezing (eg an aircraft)
Hoar frost	Water vapour in the atmosphere freezes directly onto a surface below freezing
Rime ice	A brittle layer of ice that forms on leading edges, probes etc. when an aircraft flies through cloud containing supercooled water droplets above the freezing level.
Clear ice	A sheet of ice that forms on surfaces when an aircraft flies through cloud containing supercooled water droplets above the freezing level.

Further reference: PPL3 > Meteorology > Icing

Meteorology paper 3 Q9   Answer C

The parameters of the International Standard Atmosphere (ISA) are constant regardless of location, date, air mass, weather conditions etc.

In the ISA the surface temperature is +15°C and the 'lapse rate' (the rate at which temperature decreases with altitude) is 2°C per 1000ft. Therefore, at 3,500ft the temperature is 7°C cooler (3.5 x 2) than at the surface. 15°C – 7°C = 8°C.

Further reference: PPL3 > Meteorology > The International Standard Atmosphere > The Parameters of the ISA

Meteorology paper 3 Q10   Answer C

If you think of high pressure as being like a high mountain, and low pressure as being like a low valley, it is clear that air will want to flow from high to low. 'Pressure Gradient Force' is a measure of the pressure differential over distance and the greater the pressure differential, the greater the pressure gradient force and so the faster the movement of air. The pressure gradient just like a surface gradient and you can consider isobars as being equivalent to contour lines on a map– the steeper the gradient, the closer together the lines and the quicker something will slide down it.

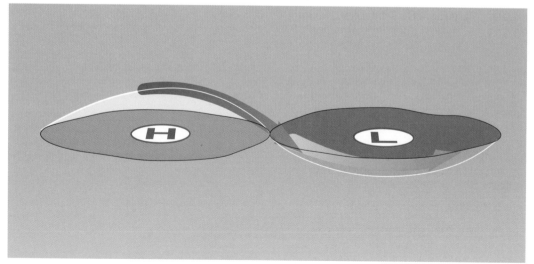

Further reference: PPL3 > Meteorology > The Motion of the Atmosphere > Pressure Gradient

Meteorology paper 3 Q11   Answer C

An anticyclone is an area of 'subsiding' – that is descending – air, hence the high pressure that defines it. As the air subsides it is compressed and warmed, which can lead to a layer of warmer air above a layer of cold air next to the surface. This is a temperature inversion – a situation where temperature remains constant or even increases with increasing height, the opposite (or inverse) of the usual situation were temperature reduces with increasing height. This is especially common in winter, when the air in the lower atmosphere is cooled by contact with the cold earth's surface.

Water, smoke and dust particles tend to become trapped below a temperature inversion, leading to a reduction in visibility over a period of days or weeks. Particularly in winter, a solid overcast of unbroken cloud may form around the inversion layer. The lack of sunlight and 'gloomy' conditions with poor visibility beneath this cloud bring around so-called 'anti-cyclonic' gloom, which may persist for several weeks during the winter in northern Europe.

Further reference: PPL3 > Meteorology > High Pressure Systems – Anticyclones and Ridges > Anticyclones

Meteorology paper 3 Q12   Answer C

An aircraft's altimeter is designed to give accurate indications in International Standard Atmosphere (ISA) conditions. Any difference between actual conditions and ISA will introduce an element of error into the altimeter reading. When that error is caused by a difference between the actual temperature and ISA temperature, a correction can be applied (altimeter temperature error correction) in order to calculate 'true' altitude. This is rarely necessary for VFR operations.

When the temperature is warmer than ISA, the altimeter will tend to under-read and the aircraft will in fact be at a higher altitude than indicated on the altimeter.

Further reference: PPL3 > Meteorology > Pressure and Altimetry > Altimetry

Meteorology paper 3 Q13   Answer B

The most common significant weather symbols used on (SIGWX) charts are found in the essential revision section: they need to be learnt.

Further reference: PPL3 > Meteorology > Aviation Weather Reports and Forecasts > Specific Forecast and Actual Formats

Meteorology paper 3 Q14   Answer D

If the aircraft has starboard (right-hand) drift, the wind must be coming from port (left-hand). According to Buys Ballot's law, in the northern hemisphere if you stand with your back to the wind, the low pressure area is on your left. Transposed onto the situation described in the question, this indicates that the aircraft is flying towards an area of low pressure.

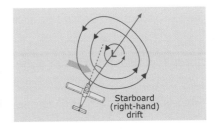

Starboard (right-hand) drift

If flying from high pressure to low pressure, without updating the altimeter setting, the aircraft will follow a constant pressure level which is, in fact, getting closer to the ground. Although the altimeter is showing a constant reading, the aircraft is in fact lower than the level indicated on the altimeter. Hence:

'High to Low, down you go'

Please note that the concept of flying any distance without updating the altimeter setting is a very dangerous one, and is emphatically <u>not</u> recommended.

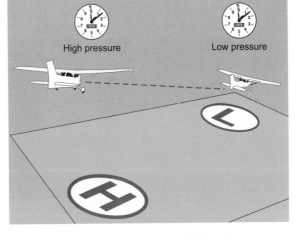

Further reference: PPL3 > Meteorology > Pressure and Altimetry > Altimetry

Meteorology paper 3 Q15   Answer C

At the position given (55N 0230E) there is no data box – remember, this is 0230<u>E</u> not 0230<u>W</u>. Therefore it is necessary to interpolate between the closest data boxes – namely those at 55N 00E and 55N 05E. The position given is half-way between each box.

The 5000ft wind at 55N 00E is 290° at 15 knots, at 55N 05E it is 280° at 20 knots. Interpolating between these figures is fairly simple, giving a mid-point of 285° at 18 knots (rounded up to the nearest knot).

There is no need to interpolate the temperature as both boxes give a figure of +01°C at 5000ft.

Remember, if your calculation gives a slightly different answer to any of the answer options, you should select the option which is closest to your calculation.

Further reference: PPL3 > Meteorology > Aviation Weather Reports and Forecasts > Specific Forecast and Actual Formats

Meteorology paper 3 Q16   Answer B

The 0°C level (in other words, the freezing level) is given as a figure representing thousands of feet above mean sea level (amsl) – see the text explanation on the left-hand side of the charts.

Further reference: PPL3 > Meteorology > Aviation Weather Reports and Forecasts > Specific Forecast and Actual Formats

Meteorology paper 3 Q17   Answer C

For a full list of met. symbols, see the Essential Revision section.

Further reference: PPL3 > Meteorology > Aviation Weather Reports and Forecasts > Specific Forecast and Actual Formats

Meteorology paper 3 Q18   Answer B

For a full list of met. symbols and METAR decode see the Essential Revision section.

On the form itself (lower left side, under chart), it is stated that "All heights are in 100s of feet above mean sea level"

Further reference: PPL3 > Meteorology > Aviation Weather Reports and Forecasts > Specific Forecast and Actual Formats

Meteorology paper 3 Q19   Answer D

For a full list of met. decodes, see the Essential Revision section.

Further reference: PPL3 > Meteorology > Aviation Weather Reports and Forecasts > Specific Forecast and Actual Formats

Meteorology paper 3 Q20   Answer C

The estimated time of departure (1300Z) is within the forecast period (1200 – 1800), but two hours before the situation depicted on the 1500 chart. This means that the warm front and associated conditions will be a further 30 miles away from the area of the navigation exercise. The conditions forecast in the exercise area are generally good visibility (25km), nil weather and broken cloud base 2500ft amsl. The reference to 2500m in mist and drizzle refers to sea and coastal areas in the N and NE of zone 1 – eg the coast of Scotland or northern England. Even in the possible isolated rain showers visibility is forecast to be no less than 10km and cloud base 2000ft amsl, which is still well within VMC limits.

All the other answer options are based on a mis-reading of METFORM215 information, for example a failure to appreciate that Zone 2 conditions will not move to cover the navigation exercise area until after the planned flight has been completed.

In real life, it would be very unwise to rely solely on an area weather forecast for making flight planning decisions. At the very least a METAR for the departure and destination airfields, and/or airfields close to the planned route, should be obtained together with any relevant aerodrome forecasts (TAF).

Further reference: PPL3 > Meteorology > Aviation Weather Reports and Forecasts > Specific Forecast and Actual Formats

	Paper 1					Paper 2					Paper 3		
	A	B	C	D		A	B	C	D		A	B	C	D
1	☐	☐	☐	☐	1	☐	☐	☐	☐	1	☐	☐	☐	☐
2	☐	☐	☐	☐	2	☐	☐	☐	☐	2	☐	☐	☐	☐
3	☐	☐	☐	☐	3	☐	☐	☐	☐	3	☐	☐	☐	☐
4	☐	☐	☐	☐	4	☐	☐	☐	☐	4	☐	☐	☐	☐
5	☐	☐	☐	☐	5	☐	☐	☐	☐	5	☐	☐	☐	☐
6	☐	☐	☐	☐	6	☐	☐	☐	☐	6	☐	☐	☐	☐
7	☐	☐	☐	☐	7	☐	☐	☐	☐	7	☐	☐	☐	☐
8	☐	☐	☐	☐	8	☐	☐	☐	☐	8	☐	☐	☐	☐
9	☐	☐	☐	☐	9	☐	☐	☐	☐	9	☐	☐	☐	☐
10	☐	☐	☐	☐	10	☐	☐	☐	☐	10	☐	☐	☐	☐
11	☐	☐	☐	☐	11	☐	☐	☐	☐	11	☐	☐	☐	☐
12	☐	☐	☐	☐	12	☐	☐	☐	☐	12	☐	☐	☐	☐
13	☐	☐	☐	☐	13	☐	☐	☐	☐	13	☐	☐	☐	☐
14	☐	☐	☐	☐	14	☐	☐	☐	☐	14	☐	☐	☐	☐
15	☐	☐	☐	☐	15	☐	☐	☐	☐	15	☐	☐	☐	☐
16	☐	☐	☐	☐	16	☐	☐	☐	☐	16	☐	☐	☐	☐
17	☐	☐	☐	☐	17	☐	☐	☐	☐	17	☐	☐	☐	☐
18	☐	☐	☐	☐	18	☐	☐	☐	☐	18	☐	☐	☐	☐
19	☐	☐	☐	☐	19	☐	☐	☐	☐	19	☐	☐	☐	☐
20	☐	☐	☐	☐	20	☐	☐	☐	☐	20	☐	☐	☐	☐

Answers

Intentionally Left Blank